About the Author

A writer. A poet. An author. A somebody to some, a nobody to most, and just enough for me.

Unsent Letters

M. B. C.

Unsent Letters

Olympia Publishers
London

www.olympiapublishers.com
OLYMPIA PAPERBACK EDITION

Copyright © M. B. C. 2024

The right of M. B. C. to be identified as author of
this work has been asserted in accordance with sections 77 and 78 of
the Copyright, Designs and Patents Act 1988.

All Rights Reserved

No reproduction, copy or transmission of this publication
may be made without written permission.
No paragraph of this publication may be reproduced,
copied or transmitted save with the written permission of the publisher,
or in accordance with the provisions
of the Copyright Act 1956 (as amended).

Any person who commits any unauthorised act in relation to
this publication may be liable to criminal
prosecution and civil claims for damage.

A CIP catalogue record for this title is
available from the British Library.

ISBN: 978-1-80439-664-3

This is a work of fiction.
Names, characters, places and incidents originate from the writer's
imagination. Any resemblance to actual persons, living or dead, is
purely coincidental.

First Published in 2024

Olympia Publishers
Tallis House
2 Tallis Street
London
EC4Y 0AB

Printed in Great Britain

Dedication

To my partner, and my best friend, thank you for being the light at the end of my tunnel. This would not have been possible without you. Thank you for showing me I could be more than my past.

Contents.

The Dawn. 13

 Broken Things. 16

 Grief. 18

 Please, stay. 20

 Flowers. 22

 My Routine. 24

 Humiliation. 26

 Anxiety. 28

 The Unsent Letter. 30

The Chaos. 33

 What did Love Look Like? 36

Promises. 38

Mother's Daughter. 40

Forbidden Fruit. 43

Sleepless Nights. 45

Questions. 48

Trigger Warning. 50

Leaving me: a Perfected Art. 53

The Dusk. 55

Why We Did Not Work. 58

My Religion. 60

My body. 62

The Women without Faces. 65

Karma. 68

Celestial Being. 70

A Familiar Feeling. 72

Maybe. 74

The Healing. 78

The Mirror I looked at. 81

What does Love Look Like Now? 84

Through the Window 86

A Sign of Healing 89

This Lifetime. 92

Long Distance. 95

My Plutonic Soulmate 97

The Girl in my Past, Woman in my Present. 100

A note to the readers. 102

The Dawn.

Broken Things.

I was told that there was something beautiful to be found in broken things.
Yet, every time I looked in the mirror, I did not see beauty back.
I saw cracks and ragged edges.
The output of a broken shape, barely being held together by good intentions and a desire for more.
I saw a hollow shell of a girl too scared to fight back.

Giving in was always easier that wanting more.
I was a shell. Mostly a pushover,
Occasionally a crying shoulder,
Undeniably a friend, And almost a lover.

Grief.

I wish I said goodbye.
I wish I was there enough to know things were that bad.
I wish I was present enough to know that you needed me and wanted me there by your side when you went to sleep for the last time.
I am so sorry, and you will never know that I was.
I still am. And I hope you know that.

I hope you know that I loved you with everything I had. And even though I was a stupid teenager too worried about my prom to realize you were fading, as a stupid adult, I see it now and wish, deeply, truly, wish – I could go back and be by your side.
There was so much life inspired by you.
There was so much love inspired by you. Our family still echoes the love you left behind.

We sit together and have dinner and although someone sits in your place now, we still keep your chair.
Your wicker chair is collecting dust in the garage because no one will ever have the heart to let it go.
It was yours. Yours to sit and have tea in every evening.
Your wicker chair, like your love, like your life, will always be with us.

Please, stay.

I begged you to stay last night.
I felt like a part of my heart was being ripped out as I tried to beg you to stay between sobs. Everyone leaves me. I could not lose you too.
I begged you, to please not do this. To please be the person you promised you would be. You promised me a forever,
you promised me you would be my forever, always.

My heart was beating, my eyes hurt, and my throat stung as I tried to mull over my words and say the right thing to get you to stay.
You asked me how I could ever trust you would stay the next time we argued – that is, if I took you back now.
I told you we would make it work because losing you, is a fate worse than death. You brought me back to life and I found myself dreaming again when you came into the picture.

You made me happy, and I could not lose that.
I never complained when people left. I let them go. I knew they would.
But I did not see it coming with you. You told me forever and always and I believed you.
I let my guard down with you. I opened my heart to you.
You said you would stay so please, I beg you, stay.

Flowers.

I remember speaking to you of the standards I set.
My poor standards where I settled for partners that could not bother to pick a weed off the ground, let alone buy me flowers.
And you chuckled. You chuckled as a tear ran down your face and you told me I was mad for selling myself so short.
That I deserved the kind of love where a man sends me different flowers every month until he figured out what my favourite kind was.
And the next day, who do I see outside my door? You.
Holding a bouquet.
You kept buying me flowers every month until you were convinced that my favourites were, indeed, sunflowers and roses.
Even when you left to chase your dreams, you sent me flowers.
I held those flowers close.

Careful to make sure they lived as long as they could, and when their time came, they were picked and pressed between my books so they could be with me even in their afterlife.

My Routine.

My insecurities choke me like an open wildfire in a house made of wood.
I try to balance on this tightrope and never outwardly show too much but it is difficult.
It is difficult to hold it in. It is difficult to limit myself to not outwardly be too much or show too much.
Too much love. Too much pain. Too much hope. Too much sorrow.
I wake up in the morning tired. Like my soul spent the majority of the night before carrying my sorrows on its back.
I begin my monotonously routine life in dread. Like my sadness is snake venom and every step I take forward, sends the poison coursing through my veins. Infecting me deeper and deeper.
I get through the day. Mostly battered and bruised.
It feels humiliating; that I struggle to cope with something everyone else finds as easy as breathing.
That's what it boils down to, doesn't it? To keep living? That's what I seem to struggle with.
Like Cinderella, the clock strikes midnight yet again and I curl myself up in bed under weighted sheets in hopes that the crushing weight will nestle me in something resembling a warm embrace.

Humiliation.

You put me in the centre of the room and let people ridicule me.
You took apart my achievements like the chalk on a pavement after a heavy rain.
You reduced my capabilities as a person, to nothing more than a hollow shell.
You spoke of my education as if it were a doomed goal from the start.
You spoke of my career like it was a pointless pursuit.

You spoke of my appearance like my body was a vessel to procreate.
Do you not see the beauty of a woman.
Instead, you see a mantlepiece. A wife. A bride. A mother.
You do not see a professional, you do not see accolades.
You do not see a person. You see a prize.
You see a keychain to coil around your finger.

The shinier, the prettier, the oh so better.
The skinnier, the taller, the oh so desirable.
Never a daughter, sometimes a prize, mostly a disappointment.

Anxiety.

I keep biting the skin on my lips. Plucking at it till it bleeds.
I keep picking at the edges of my jagged nails.
I count things – I try to maintain balance.
Twenty tiles on the bathroom floor, four colours repeating in a sequence of twenty-four vertical and thirty-six horizontals.
My friends say Hi, they normally say 'hey' – do they hate me?

I told him I loved him more than life itself – is this when he leaves?
My parents sit in silence – am I doomed to repeat history?
I look in the mirror – why do I curve in all the wrong places?
I starve my body – but I overate the other night?
The phone rings. I have fallen into a cycle of chain smoking.
"Hi, Dad, yeah, I am doing well. I just finished cooking lunch." Liar.
"Hi, guys, I would love to go out with you, but I am really busy." Liar.
"Hi, my love, I'm okay. I promise I'll tell you if I'm not." Liar.
I'll eat later. Liar. I'll be safe. Liar.
I'm happy. Liar.

The Unsent Letter.

When I was younger, none the wiser, I wrote a letter that was never sent.
A letter that dictated that I would no longer be around, and I was sorry.
Sorry that there was a battle in my mind that I was tired of fighting.
Sorry that I wanted to wave a white flag.
Sorry that I wanted it to all end.
Sorry that I wished I was stronger.
Sorry that I was tired of being a fighter.
Sorry that I struggle to sleep,
and sorry that I hated to eat.
Sorry, that despite your wishes, all I could really be, was just me.
Sorry that being me meant hurting them.
Sorry that not being me, meant losing me.
Sorry that a compromise felt like it was at the expense of my sanity.

The Chaos.

What did Love Look Like?

For the longest time, I swear I asked myself this. I was with someone for a long time. A very, very long time. I asked myself, does love look like someone who settles for me? I am chaotic and broken. Love should be someone that accepts this and lives with it. Right?
Love is someone that won't hit me or yell at me too often? Sure, he made me cry but crying wasn't so bad. Right? We cry at birth. It's a sign of life.

No. That was not love. Love cannot make me so sad, so often. Love could not be a man that demanded more out of me than I was capable of being. Love cannot be a broken piece of someone else, jammed into my cracks only to create something resembling, whole.
That could not be love. It did not feel like love. For to feel like love, it had to feel like safety. Like comfort. Like happiness.

I was not safe, or comfortable, or happy.
If anything I was miserable and suffocating

That cannot be love. That was not love.
That was denial   and a void for self-worth.

Promises.

Promises go a long way. Promises were always a bond, made to be kept and never broken.
A sacred pact, made by one soul to another, bound by pure intentions.
So if this sacred pact was made under the most dire of circumstances, why was it broken?
Why was it so easy for you to tell me you would never hurt me?
And why was it just as easy for you to break it?

Did it not haunt you? Daunt you? Pain you? To look me in the eyes as you berated me.
As you screamed at me.
As you laid your hands on me.
Did it not crush your soul and burn your heart to do that to me?
Did the embers of love you felt for me, not hold you back like sand would a fire?
Did you not sense it? Hear it? Feel it? My heart breaking.

Echoing as the pieces came crashing down and shattering into a million little pieces before you.

Mother's Daughter.

As a child, I was in a big house filled with more cousins than I could count at the time.
All unique in their own way. All developing personas that I would eventually pick and choose to mimic throughout my adulthood.
All older and much wiser, I watched them try and fail, learn and grow.
When the weight of the world was too heavy a burden, these cousins always had their mother's love to shelter and grow in.
As happy as I was to see love be received as easily as it was given, I could not help but let jealousy creep in like a vine in a garden.
Twisting, scattering, reaching and clasping to the walls of my heart.
Every time I saw my cousins get hurt, be it for their grades in an exam or a broken heart, I hurt too.

A little because it hurt to see them torn, but to my shame, it was mostly because I knew they'll be okay, eventually, when they spoke to their mothers.
Their mother would cradle them in her love.
Thirteen or thirty years of age regardless.
Their mother would comfort them with words of adoration or support or both.
Their mothers would hold them close and tell them they were

not going through this alone.

I was envious of unconditional love because I never felt it from my mother.

If anything, I felt judged. Like admitting I was hurt, or broken or needed help was the ultimate sign of weakness.

"When I was your age, I had a child," she would say.

Having a child and raising a child are two different things, Mother.

Having a child and loving a child are two different things, Mother.

Having a child and supporting a child are two different things, Mother.

At the same age you had a child, I wished I wasn't that child.

Forbidden Fruit.

You tempt a woman with an apple and expect her not to bite it.
But she does, and then she is forsaken for all eternity for an act you deemed in your eyes, as unholy?
Did you tell them the whole truth though? Everything? That you starved her? Berated her? Shamed her? Beat her? Created her void of opinion and with the sole purpose of servicing a man?

Did you warn her that to inquire, was to be damned?
That all her acts you deemed improper, were the same rights you granted to a man?
That to ask for more was impossible.
Did you tell him the same thing, I wonder.
Or did you decide that if it were him inquiring, or daring, or taking, it would be okay?

Look around you. Look at the ripple effect you created.
Women cannot walk out at night. The fruit is man.
Women cannot dress how they want. The fruit is man.
Women cannot say what they want or have autonomy over their bodies. Because, you guessed it, the fruit, is man.

Sleepless Nights.

I was read story books about monsters. Dark, grotesque creatures with sharp teeth and rotting feathers. These constructs that were just as vile inside, as they looked outside.
I was showed, clearly, that monsters looked evil. I was told, audibly, that monsters growled.
Careful to be wary of these warning signs, little me always slept with the covers over her. No matter how hot it was in the room.

I heeded the warnings I was given.
But that did not stop the dreams.
The same, twisted reoccurring dream.
He chased me, held me down and tore me apart like I was a thin sheet of paper.
I am screaming. I am fighting. I am trying to breathe, but the air is so thin. The air is running out and I am drowning.

Drowning in this sin. This evil, horrible thing.
He takes more from me than I can give.
More than I want to give.
More than I consent, to give.
This was not the monsters in the books. I was told I would be able to tell the difference between a person and a monster just by looking at them. But I could not. I did

not know the difference at that time.

You cannot expect a child to know at fifteen what she knows now at twenty-three.
I got into that car unknowingly.
I came out of it wishing for death.
I go to sleep trying to outrun it.
I wake up wishing I never had it.
My monster did not have fangs or horns. He was much smarter.
He wore a disguise. He pretended to be, family.

Innocence was taken that day.
A reoccurring nightmare was given back in exchange.

Questions.

If I told you about how the darkness in me battles the light every day, would you still stay?
Knowing you'll be with someone who is at war with herself every night?
I worry I have fallen so deep into you.
And while I sink, you are still floating.
I worry about the words exchanged in the silence between stolen glances.

I worry that, while I find the words to tell you just how much I love you, you are scrambling to find the words to let me down easy.
I worry that I love too deeply, and I worry that I let my guard down with you, even though I told myself I wouldn't do that again.
I worry that it was so easy to love you.
I worry that for you, it may not be the same.
I worry that I told you how I felt about you and that somewhere, somehow, how I feel about you, suffocated you.
I didn't want that. Please believe me.
I wanted you. Just you. As you are. Nothing more, nothing less.
But I feel like when you wanted me, you wanted less, and got too much.

Trigger Warning.

I do not think people fully understand the extent to which trauma can scar you.
Please know that survivors are not given blueprints on how to address, manage, and overcome our trauma.
Please know that I cannot afford the therapy. And even if I could, please know that I cannot afford to voluntarily relive that moment. Over and Over and Over again.

I am scared people will leave me. I am scared people will stay.
I crave for a loving touch and yet I flinch when anyone comes towards me too quickly.
I scream at night because my thoughts are plagued by the visuals of a hand holding me down while I try to break free.
My heart races when I have to walk down a road or alley alone – where is he? Is he there? Is someone else there? Are they going to get me?
This time. This time will I fight harder? Scream louder? Beg better?
Eight years and counting; yet I carry this pain like a fresh wound.
I fear uttering your name. I fear giving power to that pain. I fear images and visuals. I fear loud noises and crowded spaces.

I hurt hearing other people's stories because as much as I want to relate to the term 'survivor' – I am still trying to come to terms with the fact that I was a victim.

Leaving me: a Perfected Art.

You shut me out today.

I told you how I felt. We got into an argument and when I turned around, you were gone.

I tried calling you. You cut the line.

You finally answered. I cried. I pleaded. I begged. Between tears and stifled sobs, I told you that I was sorry. You cut the line.

It's like a sheet of rage crosses over you and you recognize nothing.

You don't recognize me.

You don't recognize love.

You don't recognize pain.

You don't recognize hurt.

How do you do it? How do you leave and stay gone, Mom? While you struggle to say 'hello' to me, I struggle to not say 'you hurt me' in return.

The Dusk.

Why We Did Not Work.

There is a fine line between being the best version of yourself;
And being someone else.
I was someone else with you. I was the version of me that you moulded to your liking.
It did not matter that I did not love her. Or even like her. You were happy to love her so long as she was the image you pictured as a child.
A broken doll for you to keep playing with.

Timid and submissive.
Bending at your call and beck.
Quiet and empty for you to occupy with your hopes and dreams.
I have always been scared of commitment; but being with you made me scared of life.
Was this all I could be? A trophy wife that was risqué enough to find hot but halal enough for you to parade around to your family?

Did you like that I stopped my writing for you?
Did you like that I gave up my voice so you could speak?
Did you like that I tried to resolve every argument before it led to screaming?
Did you like that I flinched when you raise your hand?
Or that you don't have to try hard to convince me that it was my fault all along?

My Religion.

I have had a love/hate relationship with the versions of my religion that I was raised with as a child.
I could not fathom the idea that an all-powerful being would hate what he created and would want me to suffer.
To create me with a sadness that could never be extinguished.
A void that could never be filled.
I had to stop listening to them.

The men on the speakers that echo their views of a merciless God.
God was not cruel. Not my God.
My God was kind. He forgave.
He loved.
He taught me lessons that I carry with me today.
My God was not your God even though we shared the same religion on paper.

My God was the person I prayed to and confided in during tough times.

If all else came crashing down, I had my God. And he would not judge me.

My body.

Have you ever looked in a mirror and thought that you could be more beautiful, If.
If you had longer hair.
If you had whiter teeth.
If you had a smaller waist.
If you had a prettier face.
I know I did.
I was more comfortable looking directly into the sun than in the mirror.

I was so cruel to the child that lived in this body.
I berated her, I starved her, I crushed parts of her between my fingers and wished I could smoothen them out.
I was so cruel my inner child.
But at least, no one, and I mean no one, could hurt her because the worst had already been said to her by me.
But was it fair? Was it really fair to be my own worst enemy?

I am learning to acknowledge.
Acknowledge that it was not fair.
No. It was more than unfair.
It was cruel and villainous to look at that little girl and see all the things I would change instead of appreciating all the things that she was.
God, she was smart. And funny.

She was resilient like a tumbleweed in the desert.
She was uncommonly kind, even when people didn't deserve it.
She was brave to fight her demons, every single, damn day.
Sure, she had insecurities.
And sure, everywhere she turned, longer haired, longer legged, slimmer women would strut the road and be postered up on billboards.

Praised for skipping meals because their collar bones were all the more hollow.
But this time instead of wishing she was one of them, she was happy she was her. Because that was all she ever needed to be.

The Women without Faces.

Resilience is the water.
The way she reaches for the shore. Time and time again despite being crashed against the rocks and scraping her knees on the sand.

Persistent is the ground.
Holding her fort. Standing in her place. Through landmines and hurricanes, constantly piecing together the parts of her that mankind is breaking away.

Brave is the moon.
The way she illuminates the dark with the light she steals from the sun every night. Careful to not shine too bright in fear of what she attracts in the night.

Wild is the rain.
The way she tumbles down. Charging into battle to wage wars on the ground. Sacrificing her troops to an inevitable demise.

Calm is the night.
Amidst creatures lurking under her shadow, lying in wait to hunt their unsuspecting prey.

Inquisitive is the day.

For what might today hold for her? Another war to reclaim stolen land or witnessing the birth of a child in some far-off place? Forever cursed to witness the struggle between the good and the bad, for however long she may reign.

Lost is the nature.
Her new-born leaves, forced to die in the autumn and freeze in winters. Dry up during the summers only to be reborn again during the spring. The circle of her life being taunted, repeated, day after day, night after night, all year long, for the rest of her life.

Karma.

Be careful what you do, it'll come back to you, they say.
Be careful how you act, it'll haunt you, they taunt.
Be careful how you speak, it'll bite you in the ass, they warn.
We are cautioned by the concept of Karma and all that it entails.
Karma is a spiteful woman, holding a grudge.
She is a demonic presence on holy ground.

She is a fox spirit, ready to trick you and watch you trip.
Is she really? I wonder.
I do not believe Karma is a woman waiting by the door for passers-by to fall into her clutches.
Karma is a woman cursed to balance on a tightrope.
Never to faulter, forbidden to waiver.
The world blames her for the terrible things that happen to it.

As if she did anything beyond give you, what you deserve.
She gives onto you, what you give onto others.
Karma is a not a monster. Or a temptress. Or a vixen or a trickster.
Karma is a mirror.
And just as she gives you the bad, she can give you the good. But only if you choose to be it, in the first place.

Celestial Being.

I know, despite all truths that the moon watches over us. She wears the stars like a crown or a medallion; and is armoured by the night sky.
The moon is a celestial being. A ruler of the night.
The moon is my companion. Calm. Hidden. Unnoticed.
The moon is my beacon. My reminder.

The moon is thief of the night. Syphoning the sun.
She steals the light to brighten the nights and feeds the stars to keep them alive.
The moon follows me wherever I go. Patiently behind clouds during the day, gracefully beaming through the dusky hours.

A Familiar Feeling.

I have been in the dark for so long, seeing the light felt strange.
No, it felt scary. Unfamiliar. Dangerous.
For me, unfamiliar was letting go. Familiar was running away and cutting ties and alienating myself from anything resembling happy.
Because if I could feel happy, I could feel pain.
Holding onto whatever I could that hurt me because sadness was familiar. Hurting was common.
I held on; not for the better, but for the worse. Better the devil you know, right?
I held onto people that hurt me.
I held onto vices that were bad for me.
I held onto habits that were killing me.
But the day I started letting go, oh God, it felt so good.

Giving myself the permission to be kinder to myself.
Telling myself I deserved better than this – I promise you, felt healing.
Telling myself that this too shall pass – I swear, felt safe.
Telling myself that I was worth more than my demon – most of all, felt cathartic.

Maybe.

Maybe I was not afraid to fail, maybe I was afraid to succeed.

Maybe I was not scared to love, maybe I was scared to let my guard down and be loved.

Maybe I was not weary of sleep, maybe I was frightened of dreaming.

Maybe I was not nervous of eating, maybe I was intimated by caring for my body again.

Maybe I was not alarmed by confrontation, maybe I was terrified of the truth.

Maybe I was not daunted by religion, maybe I was unnerved to believe I could be forgiven.

Maybe, I did not hate my body, maybe I just hated how the weight of other people's opinions made me feel.

Maybe I was not a bad person, maybe I just told myself that so I could justify the bad things that happened to me.

Maybe I was not hard to love, maybe I just settled for

bad people so it wouldn't hurt when they left.

Maybe I was not a broken person, maybe I was just made to feel like damaged goods.

Maybe I was not soft, maybe I was caring enough to not be a part of the problem.

Maybe I am not the labels they give me.

Maybe I am not the problem.

Maybe, I don't need to be saved.

Maybe, just maybe, I am happy with who I am.

The Healing.

The Mirror I looked at.

My mind was never an easy thing to unravel.
I would cry myself to sleep like I had a quota to finish and then would wake up empty.
I wanted, so desperately, to be more than what I was.
I wanted, so desperately, to be something resembling happy.
I could not tackle my mind so instead I tackled my body.

I hate what I put her through. I really do.
She supported me and held me when I cried alone.
She was the only one that wiped my tears when everyone else thought I was taking a shower.
My body was my holy grounds and instead of worshipping her like a temple, I threw stones at her.
I looked at her and felt disgust when I should have seen bravery.

My body had stretch marks in awkward places like my thighs and my arms.
I hated them. But I look at them now, and I think;
Look at how you have grown, little poet.
Look at how you are no longer weak and pale.
Look at how the white woman tans to be your colour.
Look at how the sun glistens on your brown skin.

Look at how your black hair absorbs the heat and radiates warmth.

Look at how you smile.

It is not a smile forced; it is a smile felt.

What does Love Look Like Now?

Love is kind.
Love is patient and wholesome.
Love is asking me if I got home and how my day was.
Did you eat?
How did you sleep?
Tell me about what's bothering you.
I am here for you.
Hearing someone cares, and looking into their eyes are seeing that they genuinely meant it; was love.

'Good morning, beautiful' he whispered to me every day.
'How are you, my love?' he asked with inquisitive eyes.
He said his eyes were brown and boring, but I looked at him and saw warm honey and burnt sugar.
Ripples of hazel through dark streaks of black.
Looking into his eyes, I saw concern and adoration.

I saw acceptance and kindness.

I saw curiosity and catharsis.

Love is not a person; it is a feeling.

But my God, did this person come so close to being love.

Through the Window.

How do I begin to describe the only man that has
made me see colours in a soul. Soft hues of hazel
against honey.
How do I begin to find the words to tell him that
loving him felt as easy as breathing.
Falling for him was like rain,
Begin held by him felt like coming home,
Hearing his voice felt like safety,

How do I tell this man that I felt like a fading ember all
my life until he came along like pouring gasoline.
Overflowing at the seams.
That he started a wildfire in me that burned so bright,
That lit up the night,
That inspired a fight.
How do I tell him that I felt like an outcast. An outsider
always looking in through double glazed windows at what life
could have been.

How do I tell him that all of that changed with a look on
his face and the actions he paved.
He opened the door, and gave me his clothes,
and he told me to come in from the blistering cold.
And when I asked him how long I could stay,
He told me that this could be home.
That I was never alone.

And there was no need to stand by the door.
He told me that I was free to go, but if I ever needed home, or a place to shelter from the cold, I could always come home.

A Sign of Healing.

I did something for myself today.
I mixed honey with tea, like the thick golden treacle would somehow heal my soul.
I had a bath, like the scalding hot water would wash away my sorrows like waves wash away debris.
I read a book, like the words would blanket me in their warm embrace like a friend would after years of being apart.

I watered my plants, like their growth would somehow inspire the sprouts of happiness in me to grow.
I folded my clothes, like organizing them would somehow help me compartmentalize pieces of my sadness in neat little sections, to open when I'm ready.
While it may not seem like much, it was a battle.
To wake up, herd all my sadness like a farmer would his flock and move them to greener pastures.
To wake up and choose to be productive.
To not give my sadness an open floor to seek refuge.
To not give my sadness the chance to dance around in my room, echoing their dark words of self-deprecation and woeful misery.
To not give my sadness an opportunity to gather around the campfire that was my hopes and dreams and tell stories around

it as my happiness faded from flames to embers, eventually to ash.
No, today I did not do that. Today, I chose to do something else.
And dare I say, I think I won a long-lost battle.
Maybe one day, I will attempt the war.

This Lifetime.

How is it that I learn new things about you every day, but I feel as if I have known you for a lifetime?
How is it that when we are together it feels like a twin flame that has been burning far before the two of us – and will keep burning far after.
Do you believe in fate? I didn't.
But I have this theory. That Zeus was right all along.

That our souls, that were once whole, are now two halves, forced to be apart – searching throughout the days, and despite the nights; for each other.
And in every lifetime that we met, we fell in love with the histories of the last, and the depth of the present.
My theory is that in every lifetime we spent together, even if it hurt to lose you, I knowingly still chose to look for you all over again in the next.

Because any lifetime with you, even a glimpse, even a linger, was worth more than the days that preceded you.
I do not know how long we had in our other lifetimes, nor of the lives we led in them.
I do not know how long we have in this lifetime, nor of the lives we will lead in this.
I do know, however, that meeting you felt like it was a long-time coming.

Like the past caught up with the present and intertwined.
Like the histories we have shared collided.
I do know, that I will love you for however long we have in this life and even more so, I will find you in the next.

Long Distance.

There are oceans between us. There are cities we have not trekked and roads we have not travelled between us.
We are an eight-hour plane ride apart and I see you in person less in a year than I would my doctor for a check-up.
I long for the chance to tell you goodnight in person and not through a screen.
But make no mistake, there is not a moment that goes by where my heart does not ache for yours and my hands do not wish to feel your warmth.
There are no words in the English language to describe the depth that I feel for you.
Being with you feels like coming home. Everyday.
Fighting with you feels like getting through a hurdle together. Never apart.
How different it is, to love your best friend.

To find your person and be sure that if all else fails, if the world were to fall apart in this very moment, I have lived a full life by being loved so all-consumingly by you.

My Plutonic Soulmate.

Hello, you, my soulmate. We are not lovers but my how we are friends for life.
You carry my sorrows and answer my calls at three a.m. when I am crying.
How beautiful you are, both inside and out.
You water my garden and watch as the flowers bloom.
There is a tandem of joy and sadness in your heart that could have only been brought upon by past sorrows and sickly-sweet memories.

You do not let that hold you back though, if anything, you use it to fuel a fire in you.
Oh, how you inspire me, dear best friend. You show me how beautiful life can be by your sheer resilience in the harshest of climates.
You are as resilient as the weeds that grow on a sidewalk.
You are bright as the sun itself.
You are as strong as the hurdles you overcame.

I cannot say for certain how you do it, I cannot pretend at best, to understand it.
But oh, can I admire the beauty you exude. And oh, can I watch the path you have created for yourself.
This world is a labyrinth and to watch you navigate, through thick and thin, bitter and sweet, these uncharted territories.

How beautiful it is to see you blossom.

How incredible it is, to see you grow.

How inspirational it is, to see you love.

So fierce, so bold, so beautiful, so wise.

I want to protect your heart, that you give to the fullest to those you care for. I want to cherish, the trust you cascade. I want to protect, the love you share.
But most of all, I want to walk alongside you on this journey, because although we are not bound by blood, you have always been my family.

The Girl in my Past, Woman in my Present.

There is a child I left in the past that comes back from time to time and tries to convince me she was unloved.
She screams at me to give her attention because she never truly got any as a child.
She is banging at pots and pans and pleading with me to believe her when she says she's alone.
There is an adult in my present that is speaking to her and telling her she should have been loved, and is loved, now.
The woman gives her the attention she needs to process her pain and acknowledge her closure.
Holding her close. Tight. Not letting go.
There is an exchange of words being uttered without a single word being spoken.
It was not fair then, and it is not fair now.
But, I am here for you now.

And, you are not alone.
I will not fight you; I am trying to save you.
For better or worse, I love you.

A note to the readers.

I wrote these words as an attempt to put my emotions onto paper.
To give my sadness a place to seek refuge and give my mind a chance to grow beyond my past.
I do not know for certain if any of what you read will resonate with you, but I sincerely thank you for coming on this journey with me.

Please know that this journey, although put into four neat categories, was far from neat or methodical.
Some days I am a mixture of all of them, others, none.
So regardless of if you are in your Dawn, Chaos, Dusk, or healing – all of the above, or none, please know that you are not alone.
You serve a purpose. The purpose to live and be who you are.
Whoever that may be.